QUILTER'S

YEAR

BOOK

52 weeks to explore
your inner quilt genius
and have some fabric fun

Published in 2016 by Lucky Spool Media, LLC

Lucky Spool Media, LLC
1005 Blackwood Lane, Lafayette, CA 94549
www.luckyspool.com
info@luckyspool.com

TEXT BY: Samarra Khaja © Lucky Spool Media, LLC.
EDITOR: Susanne Woods
ASSISTANT EDITOR: Kari Vojtechovsky
ILLUSTRATIONS: Kari Vojtechovsky (except where noted)
PHOTOGRAPHY: © Lauren Hunt (except where noted)
DESIGNER: Kari Vojtechovsky

Photography on page 67 © Erin Cox; pages 33, 107 © Holly De Groot;
pages 44, 90 © Cindy Derby; page 18 © Amy Gibson; page 29 © Paula Pepin;
page 3 © Ann Price; page 43 © Jade Smithard; and pages 12, 65 © Gale Zucker.

Illustrations on page 61 © Alison Glass.

9 8 7 6 5 4 3 2 1
First Edition
Printed and bound in China

Library of Congress Cataloging-in-Publication Data available upon request

ISBN: 978-1-940655-24-6

LSID 0026

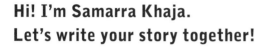

Hi! I'm Samarra Khaja.
Let's write your story together!

Welcome to 52 weeks of inspiration! I want to help you tell your own story, have some fun with your fabric, push you to try new things and keep track of a year's worth of progress inside this journal. Here's how it works:

Each week, I'll give you an idea, a challenge, or a goal to achieve. Sometimes you will be able to complete the journal entry within a week, others are more long-range plans that you will have to come back to and write about a few weeks later when you have completed the challenge. At the end of 52 weeks, I think you'll see a whole new you! Together, we'll tackle your sewing space and your fabric stash, we'll try new and exciting fabric combinations and paste in your current favorites. We'll go to new places and try new things. We'll even leave secret messages for your friends and family to help fuel your sensational sewing!

Why the Quilter's Yearbook? Because just like those dusty high school yearbooks tucked up in your attic somewhere, this journal will highlight your favorite things, your best friends, your life's moments and your predictions for the future you. And the best part? You'll look back at this Yearbook in the years to come wondering why that was your favorite fabric in just the same way as you now question that Flock of Seagulls haircut that was so cool back in the 80's.

Yup—this is going to be fun! So buckle up for 52 weeks folks, this is going to be quite a ride!

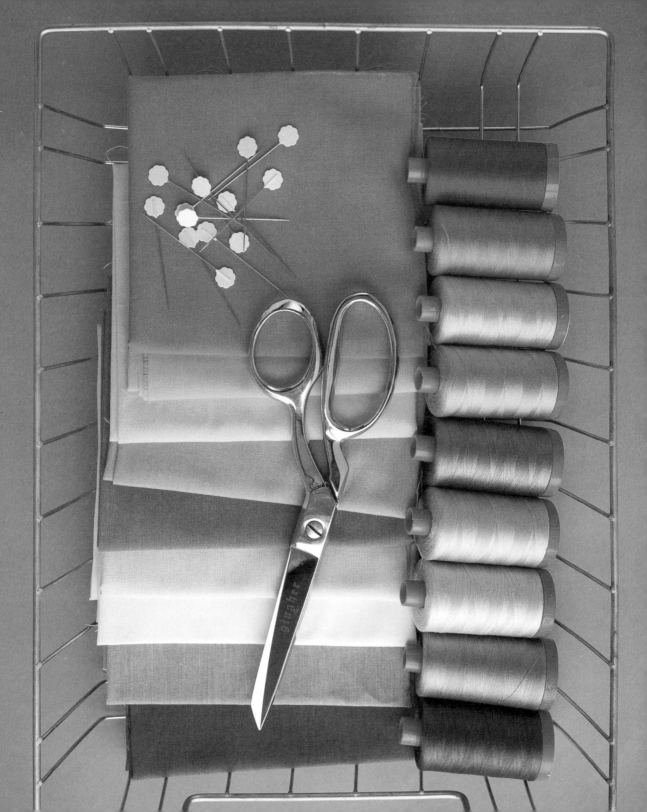

EAGER TO DIVE IN?

Me too. But wait, first, let's make this journal all your own and stock it with all of the tools you'll need to complete 52 weeks of fun.

After all, you'll want to be able to tell which yearbook is which when you get together with all of your sewing friends who also have their own copy of this journal...and you'll need to be able to tell them apart.

To complete most of the challenges each week, you'll need a pencil or pen, a pair of scissors and a glue stick. Are you a rule follower who was taught never to write in books? Well throw off those chains of creativity and let's sew through this cover shall we??!

Here is a quick project that will keep all of your supplies to hand, customize your journal and loosen up your fear of filling this journal with glue, thread, fabric, stitches and maybe some secrets too.

MATERIALS:

(1) 10" x 18" strip of your favorite fabric

iron

water-soluble marker

sewing machine fitted with a leather needle

Keep it close, keep it closed! Here's how:

ASSEMBLING THE FABRIC STRIP

1. Set your stitch length to 2.0 or a slightly smaller stitch length than usual

2. Fold your fabric strip in half, wrong sides together. Press. (Fig. a)

FIGURE A.

3. Open up the pressed fabric and fold the edges of the fabric strip, wrong sides together to meet at the middle crease from Step 2 (Fig. b). Fold in half again, encasing the raw edges. Press.

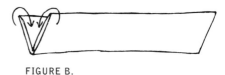

FIGURE B.

4. Topstitch along both long edges of the pressed strip. (Fig. c)

5. Fold one short raw edge of the pressed strip by ½" and press (Fig. d). Repeat for the remaining short raw edge.

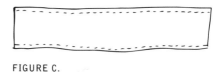

FIGURE C.

6. Using a soluable marker, or any other removable marking instrument, mark vertical lines on the right side of the strip at the following measurements from the right edge:
2½", 3½", 5⅝", 7¼", and 11¾".

FIGURE D.

7. Open the journal cover so that only the front cover is on your work surface.

8. Position the sewn strip on the aqua bar printed on the front journal cover with one pressed ½" tab fold at the right edge of the cover. Stitch scant ⅛" in from right edge of the cover to secure the sewn fabric strip. (Fig. e)

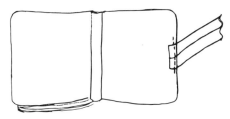

FIGURE E.

9. Open the journal cover so that only the back cover is on your work surface. Position the sewn strip on the back journal cover and repeat Step 8 for the left edge. Be careful not to twist the strip and make sure the elastic closure is inside back cover and out of the way. (Fig. f)

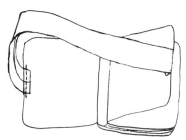

FIGURE F.

10. Align the marked lines from Step 6 with the corresponding printed lines on the cover. Being careful to avoid the elastic closure, sew the supply dividers through the strip and the front or back covers. There will be some slack in each divider to allow room for your tools. (Fig. g)

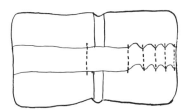

FIGURE G.

11. Load up your journal with your supplies!

Your Next Best Quilt

Your mind is a treasure trove of greatness, so let's pour some of that out onto this page with a list of your favorite quilt patterns that you have yet to make. Attach a photo of each and write about the one you're going to tackle next.

Up Next!

Attach Photo Here

PATTERN NAME, DESIGNER & PLANS FOR MAKING MY VERSION:

WHY I CHOSE THIS QUILT PATTERN:

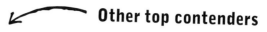 **Other top contenders**

Attach Photo Here

Attach Photo Here

Attach Photo Here

PATTERN NAME & DESIGNER:

....

....

PATTERN NAME & DESIGNER:

....

....

PATTERN NAME & DESIGNER:

....

....

Attach Photo Here

Attach Photo Here

Attach Photo Here

PATTERN NAME & DESIGNER:

....

....

PATTERN NAME & DESIGNER:

....

....

PATTERN NAME & DESIGNER:

....

....

Block-splosion

Woohoo, time to show these pages who's boss and finish these block designs!

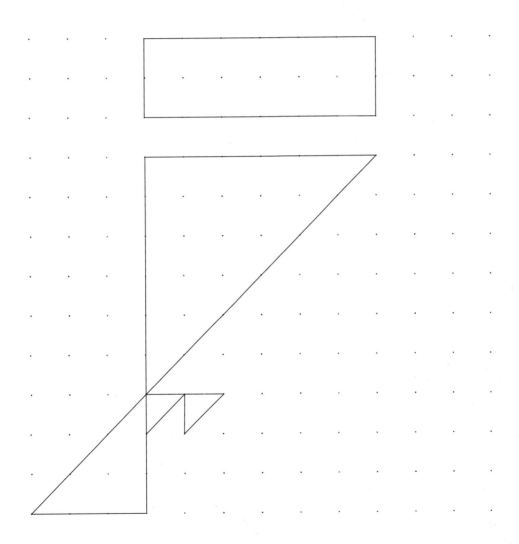

Top of the Class

Write about which quilt maker you would really want to take a class with
the most and why? And if you could gain any skills by osmosis, what knowledge
of theirs would you most love to absorb?

four Playing Favorites

Surely there's an old adage out there that sagely reminds us that "'Tis never wise to play favorites amongst children, but perfectly fine to do so with fabric!" With that green light approval, go through your fabric stash and list out your current top 10 fave fabrics and attach a swatch for each one here. Write a little bit about what makes it a favorite: Why you like this fabric, where you bought it, or even whether you liked it right away or if it had to grow on you for a while. If you aren't completing this for the first time, take a look at this page from a prior Yearbook. Anything changed?

Attach Swatch Here

WHY I LOVE THIS FABRIC:

....

....

....

Attach Swatch Here

WHY I LOVE THIS FABRIC:

....

....

....

Attach Swatch Here

WHY I LOVE THIS FABRIC:

....

....

....

Attach Swatch Here

WHY I LOVE THIS FABRIC:

....

....

....

Attach Swatch Here

Attach Swatch Here

Attach Swatch Here

WHY I LOVE THIS FABRIC:

WHY I LOVE THIS FABRIC:

WHY I LOVE THIS FABRIC:

Attach Swatch Here

Attach Swatch Here

Attach Swatch Here

WHY I LOVE THIS FABRIC:

WHY I LOVE THIS FABRIC:

WHY I LOVE THIS FABRIC:

Prized Posession

Spill the beans, what's your most prized possession in your home? Paste a picture of it here. Think you can turn it into an appliqué or an embroidery? Use the page opposite to draw it out.

Designer Dreaming

Rapid-fire question time: If you designed your very own fabric line, what color palette would you choose? What would your collection's theme be? What would you call your line? And the cherry on top of this sundae of fabric scrumptiousness: what would your selvage look like?

My Color Palette

COLLECTION NAME:

THEME:

My Selvage

Doing Good (Really Good)

Brace yourself, because there are some stellar karma points to be gained here: Create a simple quilt top and gift it to a favorite charity. Write here about that experience.

CHARITY NAME: ....

DATE GIVEN: ....

WHAT DID MAKING A QUILT AND GIVING IT TO THE CHARITY FEEL LIKE?

....

....

....

....

....

....

....

....

....

Attach Photo of
Quilt Top Here

QUILT NAME:

New and Notable Notion

It's time to shove you out of your comfort zone: Borrow or buy a tool or a notion that you've never tried before and give it a whirl. Write about what you chose and how you liked it.

NOTION TRIED: ....

DATE: ....

PRICE: ....

STARS: ☆☆☆☆☆

DID IT WORK AS PROMISED? WAS IT HELPFUL? WILL YOU USE IT AGAIN? DETAILS PLEASE!

....

....

....

....

....

....

....

....

Fear and Loathing in Your Sewing Room

Time to face The Scary head-on: What technique are you most afraid of trying? After breathing slowly into a paper bag to calm down, write here about what would help take away the intimidation and replace it with brave go-getter-y-ness (because if we can invent our own words, we can surely tackle this technique!)

One Word: De-stash.
We Know, We Know, Deep Breaths...

Thoughtfully go through your fabrics and make a stack of keepers, a stack of "It's not me, it's you" lovelies and a stack of "I have no idea what I was thinking" brainfart acquisitions (we all have those). Happily re-home those last two categories of fabric by way of sale, swap or donation.

I am keeping these 3 fabrics until my dying day
(or the perfect project, whichever comes first...)

Attach Swatch Here	Attach Swatch Here	Attach Swatch Here

FABRIC COLLECTION:

....

FABRIC COLLECTION:

....

FABRIC COLLECTION:

....

WHY I'LL NEVER GIVE IT UP:

WHY I'LL NEVER GIVE IT UP:

WHY I'LL NEVER GIVE IT UP:

?? o ?

The craziest "not me" fabric I de-stashed.

Attach Swatch Here

Results:

☐ I made out like a bandit selling my old fabrics for a total of $ ....

☐ I paid forward good fabric karma by donating my fabric to ....

☐ You don't expect me to actually get rid of fabric, do you?

CLEANING OUT MY STASH MADE ME FEEL...

The Digital Frontier

Voyage into the unknown; it's really not that scary: Try an online quilting class or join the Mighty Lucky Quilting Club (www.luckyspool.com/mightylucky). Go on, sign up and jump in. If you're feeling unsure, use a pithy alias for added entertainment; suggestions include 'Sensai Craftastic' and 'Commander Quilticus the Third'. Write here about the experience and what your favorite takeaway tip was!

CLASS TAKEN: ....

PLATFORM: ....

FAVORITE TIP: ....

....

....

....

REVIEW: ....

....

....

....

My epic user name:

....

twelve

The Lucky Seven

You know those quilts that make your heart skip a beat when you see them:
List and attach a photo for each of your 7 top favorite quilt patterns EVER.
If you haven't already made them, which lucky one will you gleefully
conquer next?

#1. QUILT NAME & DESIGNER:

....

☐ Made it   ☐ Will make it   ☐ Will make several

Attach Photo Here

Attach Photo Here

#2. QUILT NAME & DESIGNER:

....

☐ Made it   ☐ Will make it   ☐ Will make several

#3. QUILT NAME & DESIGNER:

....

☐ Made it   ☐ Will make it   ☐ Will make several

Attach Photo Here

Attach Photo Here

#4. QUILT NAME & DESIGNER:

☐ Made it   ☐ Will make it   ☐ Will make several

#5. QUILT NAME & DESIGNER:

Attach Photo Here

☐ Made it   ☐ Will make it   ☐ Will make several

Attach Photo Here

#6. QUILT NAME & DESIGNER:

☐ Made it   ☐ Will make it   ☐ Will make several

#7. QUILT NAME & DESIGNER:

Attach Photo Here

☐ Made it   ☐ Will make it   ☐ Will make several

Slow Jam

Let's slow things down a bit and try a small handwork project. Pick something enjoyably relaxing; think English paper piecing, appliqué, broderie perse (hello, totally the name of my next garage band) and hand quilting.

WHAT DID YOU CHOOSE TO MAKE AND WOULD YOU DO IT AGAIN ON A LARGER SCALE?

Attach Photo or
Sample Here

Pro tip: Have copious amounts of chocolate at the ready.

fourteen

Creative Block

You're made of pure magic! Show it by finishing these block designs!

The Hook Up

List your 10 favorite stores to buy fabric and write a wishlist of what you'd want from each place. Use this trusty bookmark to do your gift-hinting dirty work. Just fill it in and leave it somewhere obvious; squarely in the middle of the bathroom mirror is pretty subtle and effective.

Hey, ... !

What's this, you ask? Just the most unassuming and crazy-helpful list of my favorite fabric stores (like you didn't already know) and what I'd adore to have from each of them. You know, in case any upcoming gift needs arise. You're welcome!

Sincerely, ...

#1. FABRIC STORE: ....

ADDRESS OR URL ....

WHAT I NEED: ....

....

....

....

#2. FABRIC STORE: ....

ADDRESS OR URL ....

WHAT I NEED: ....

....

....

....

#3. FABRIC STORE: ....

ADDRESS OR URL ....

WHAT I NEED: ....

....

....

....

#4. FABRIC STORE: ....

ADDRESS OR URL ....

WHAT I NEED: ....

....

....

....

#5. FABRIC STORE: ....

ADDRESS OR URL ....

WHAT I NEED: ....

....

....

....

Book Worm

What's your top 10 list of books? Feel free to write *Quilter's Yearbook*
in at number one and add a spot for an entry for an 11th title at the bottom.
So accommodating we are, hardy har har!

List of Books:

#1. ....

#2. ....

#3. ....

#4. ....

#5. ....

#6. ....

#7. ....

#8. ....

#9. ....

#10. ....

#11. ....

Free Your Motion

Turn up your favorite jam. Okay, louder... LOUDER! Good. Now, let the sounds immerse that ever-so-creative brain of yours and draw a quilting design based on that song! Jam on it!

This quilting design brought to you courtesy of the song:

I've Got a Notion

Assuming the answer is not 'donuts', although it clearly should be, what are your favorite sewing tools or notions right now? List those bad boys here! Booyah!

Quilt Making Isn't Any Fun Without:

#1.

#2.

#3.

#4.

#5.

#6.

#7.

#8.

#9.

#10.

nineteen

Thumbs Down

What's your least favorite fabric combination? Without dry heaving, put swatches of them here. Hold my hand, this may make us both light-headed. What could possibly help this vision play a bit more nicely together?

Attach Swatch Here

+

Attach Swatch Here

= yuck!

WHAT COULD MAKE IT WORK:

```
┌·······················┐   ┌·······················┐
:                       :   :                       :
:                       :   :                       :
:                       :   :                       :
:   Attach Swatch Here  : + :   Attach Swatch Here  :   = ew, gross
:                       :   :                       :
:                       :   :                       :
:                       :   :                       :
└·······················┘   └·······················┘
```

WHAT COULD MAKE IT WORK:

....

....

```
┌·······················┐   ┌·······················┐
:                       :   :                       :
:                       :   :                       :
:                       :   :                       :
:   Attach Swatch Here  : + :   Attach Swatch Here  :   = my eyes hurt
:                       :   :                       :
:                       :   :                       :
:                       :   :                       :
└·······················┘   └·······················┘
```

WHAT COULD MAKE IT WORK:

....

....

Blocks of Time

Time to finish another couple of quilt blocks! Try doing each of these at a different time of the day—one early in the morning and the other late at night—for some fun comparing and contrasting your completed work.

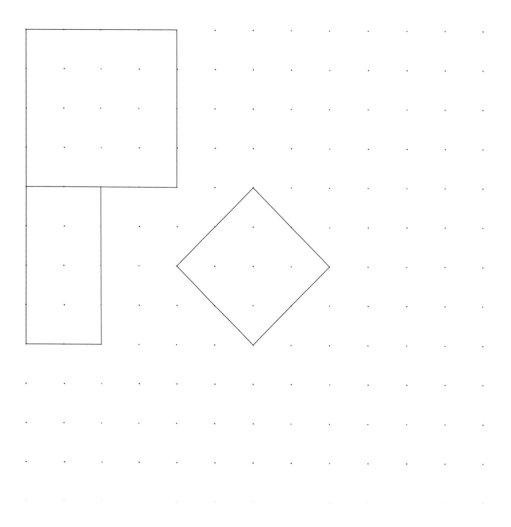

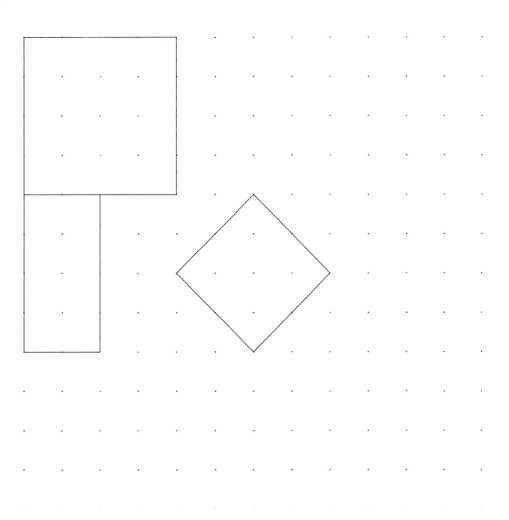

twenty one

Soak In the Quilty Goodness

Because it's always good to get out and enjoy the world, gussy yourself up
(look, if that means a fresh pair of yoga pants, then that it shall be!)
and attend a local quilt show.

SHOW VISITED: ....

DATE: ....

I'D RATHER: ☐ Still be there   ☐ Change my rotary blade   ☐ Have a root canal

WHAT DID YOU GET INSPIRED BY? FIND SOMETHING YOU'VE NEVER SEEN BEFORE? MAKE ANY PURCHASES?

....

....

....

....

....

....

....

....

twenty two

Quilting Rules!

Okay, you clever, adaptable thing, you. Time to borrow or buy a ruler you've never tried before. Write down some of the things you first read about that ruler and what you've since learned after using it.

RULER TRIED: ....

DATE: ....

PRICE: ....

STARS: ☆ ☆ ☆ ☆ ☆

WHAT PROJECT DID YOU USE IT ON? WAS THE RULER COOLER OR A DROOLER?

....

....

....

....

....

....

....

....

Release Your Inner Quilt Genius

Okay, you've walked around with it rattling around in your brain long enough. Time to get that great quilt design out of your glorious noggin and onto this paper. Annnd, go!

twenty
four

Can You See What I'm Saying?

Okay, so basically synesthesia is a neurological phenomenon in which stimulation of one sensory/cognitive pathway leads to automatic, involuntary experiences in a second sensory/cognitive pathway. Given that, choose a fabric that evokes your favorite fragrance or flavor. Start with one fabric and add to it, making a 'yummy' smell/taste-inspired fabric palette.

FLAVOR/SCENT
INSPIRATION: ....

INSPIRING COLORS: ....

....

....

....

INSPIRING TEXTURES: ....

....

....

....

....

....

Attach Swatch Here

Attach Swatch Here

Attach Swatch Here

Attach Swatch Here

Attach Swatch Here

Attach Swatch Here

Attach Swatch Here

Binder Full

Do you keep pages from magazines, postcards, or other random reference pieces for future pattern and quilt inspiration? Time to go through those papers and toss what no longer lights your fire. Keep the ones that do, and organize them into a sweet binder of future success. Did you rediscover long-lost faves? How many did you purge? And did you find any that have bounced up to the top of your to-make list?

Long-lost Faves Rediscovered:

Make pronto!

#1. .... ☐

#2. .... ☐

#3. .... ☐

#4. .... ☐

#5. .... ☐

I GOT RID OF THIS MANY PATTERNS AND I'M NOT LOOKING BACK!

THE BEST THING ABOUT CLEANING OUT MY PATTERN STASH:

twenty six

Creative License

if you could create your own sewing-related license plate, what would it say? Extra points given for painfully good groan-worthy puns.

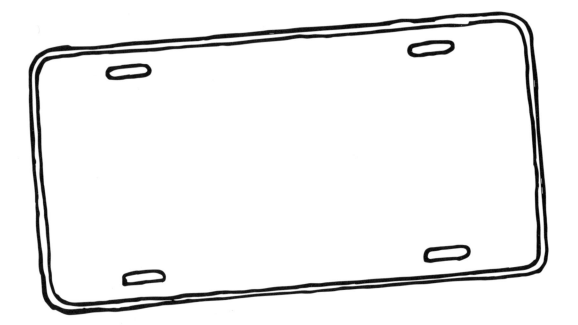

Share yours on Instagram using **#QUILTERSYEARBOOK**

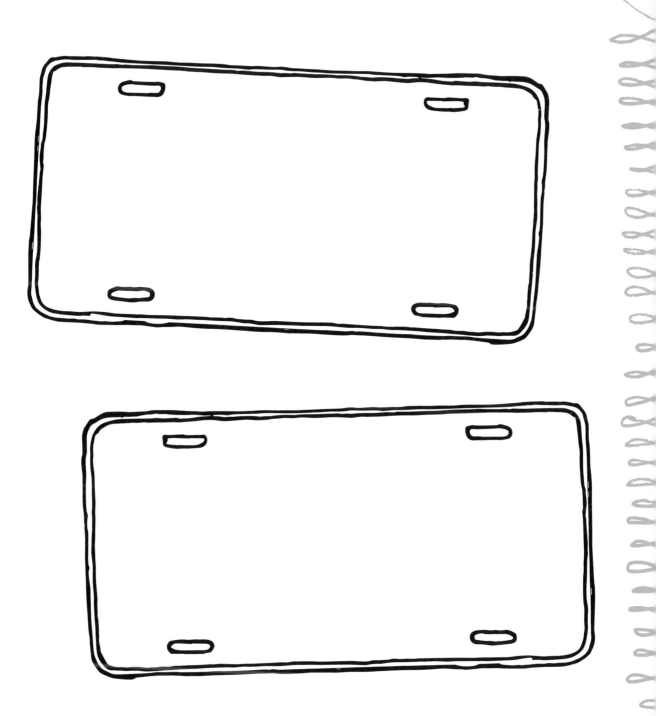

twenty seven

Floss Boss

Using these basic stitches along with an iron-on embroidery transfer, create your own custom embroidery pattern. Attach a strand of each different floss color you used here and smile at your inherent greatness!

PATTERN NAME: ....

DATE: ....

My Pretty Floss Palette:

Embroidery Stitch Quick Guide

RUNNING STITCH

SATIN STITCH

STRAIGHT STITCH

CHAIN STITCH

FEATHER STITCH

BACKSTITCH

CROSS STITCH

BASIC HERRINGBONE STITCH

SHEAF STITCH

twenty eight

Be a Block Head

Ta-da! Exercise those fabu brain muscles and finish these block designs!

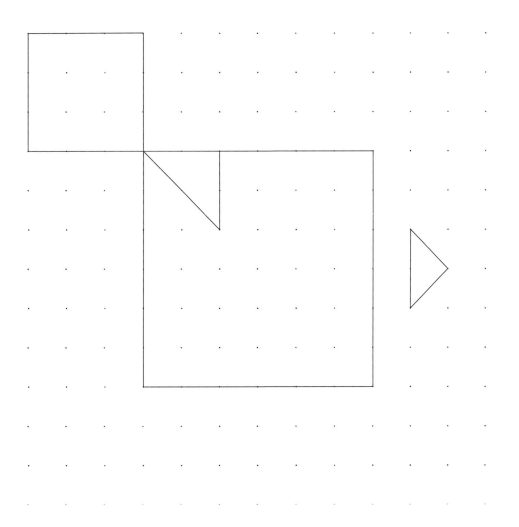

twenty nine

Find Your Tribe

Unfurl your social butterfly wings and attend a local quilt guild meeting!
Mix it up by going to a modern one if you're already part of a traditional guild
or vice versa. Bring festive snacks! Write about the experience here.

GUILD VISITED: ....

DATE: ....

I'LL BE BACK: ☐ Next meeting   ☐ Someday   ☐ Not in a million years

MY EXPERIENCE AT THE GUILD:

....

....

....

....

....

....

....

....

Swap It Challenge

Okay, so hold onto your hat because this is a fun one: Pick your favorite go-to pattern and ask a sewing friend to pick theirs and then, wait for it, swap patterns and make a quilt top based on theirs! It gets better: now gift that finished quilt back to your friend, huzzah! Or if you both prefer, agree to donate both your finished quilts to a favorite charity. This has warm and fuzzy written all over it!

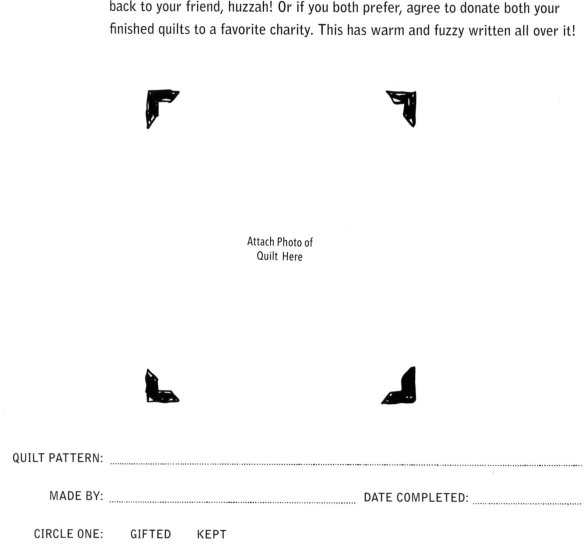

Attach Photo of
Quilt Here

QUILT PATTERN: ....

MADE BY: .... DATE COMPLETED: ....

CIRCLE ONE: GIFTED   KEPT

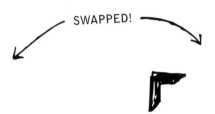

SWAPPED!

Attach Photo of
Quilt Here

QUILT PATTERN: ....

MADE BY: .... DATE COMPLETED: ....

CIRCLE ONE: GIFTED   KEPT

thirty
one

Read All About It

Come on, Captain BiblioPants, time to borrow or buy a sewing book that you've never read before. What book was it and how did you like it? Share here!

TITLE: ....

AUTHOR: ....

DATE: ....

PRICE: ....

STARS: ☆ ☆ ☆ ☆ ☆

THOUGHTS? ANY NEW TIPS, TECHNIQUES OR PATTERNS YOU PICKED UP?

....

....

....

....

....

....

....

....

thirty two

Trip the Light Scraptastic

Your fabric scraps will surely thank you because it's time to make a mini quilt! Challenge yourself to try a new technique or work in a style that isn't usual for you, using a favorite book or specific pattern as your guide. Attach a photo of both the pattern and the finished quilt here. Marvel at how amazing you are!

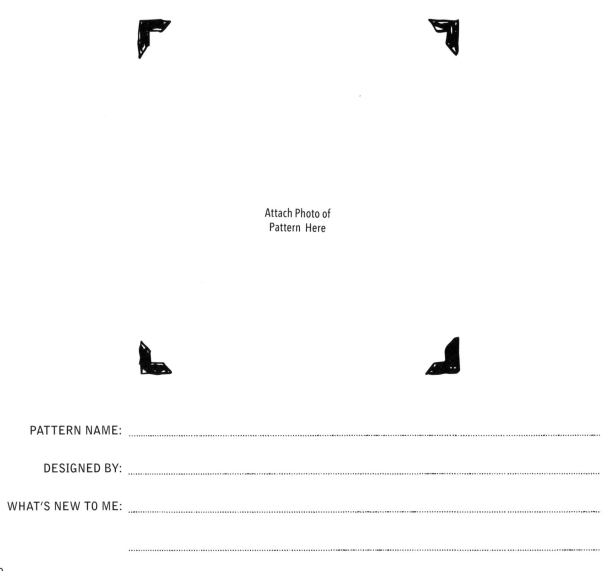

Attach Photo of
Pattern Here

PATTERN NAME: ....

DESIGNED BY: ....

WHAT'S NEW TO ME: ....

....

Attach Photo of
Finished Quilt Here

QUILT NAME: ....

DATE COMPLETED: ....

THOUGHTS: ....

....

thirty three

Time Machine

Find swatches of 3 different fabrics that have lived in your stash for a very long time; attach them to the right and write down their approximate purchase dates. Now do the same with 3 fabrics you just bought.

Think all 6 fabrics could work together or should they really be kept apart for their own good?

☐ Hey, these fabrics look pretty great together!

☐ Hmm... not my favorite combination but I could make it work if I had to.

☐ These fabrics go together like oil and water.

COMPARE THE OLDER CHOICES WITH YOUR NEWEST ONES. WHICH DO YOU LIKE MORE?
HAVE YOUR TASTES CHANGED OR ARE THEY STILL SIMILAR?

The Oldies But Goodies

Attach Swatch Here

Attach Swatch Here

Attach Swatch Here

APPROX. PURCHASE DATE:

APPROX. PURCHASE DATE:

APPROX. PURCHASE DATE:

The New Additions

Attach Swatch Here

Attach Swatch Here

Attach Swatch Here

APPROX. PURCHASE DATE:

APPROX. PURCHASE DATE:

APPROX. PURCHASE DATE:

thirty four

Appliqué, Okay?

We're going to layer up our fun now: first, finish up these block designs. Then, add an appliqué design over the top of each finished block for extra eye candy pizazz. Congratulate yourself on this marvelous work with some celebratory jazz hands!

Tool Many

We know your creative cup runneth over, but we also don't want you to get buried under it. Survey your sewing space for surplus stuff (whoa, say THAT ten times fast). Choose 10 things to donate or discard in order to free up mental and physical space. What did you get rid of? And how do you feel now?

I Let Go of:

#1.

#2.

#3.

#4.

#5.

#6.

#7.

#8.

#9.

#10.

NOT HAVING THESE IN MY LIFE IS LIKE:

thirty six

Show Off

Let's unlock that next level of Quiltlandia (patent-pending) and enter a quilt into a quilt show! Yup, really. The key is not to overthink it and to jump in; write about it here. CANNONBALL!

QUILT SHOW: ....

DATE: ....

RESULTS: ....

HOW DO YOU FEEL ABOUT ENTERING YOUR WORK FOR SHOW? WILL YOU DO IT AGAIN?

....

....

....

....

....

....

....

....

Attach Photo of
Quilt Here

QUILT NAME: ....

SIZE: .... DATE COMPLETED: ....

OTHER DETAILS: ....

....

Feeling It

Draw a quilting design with your eyes closed! But not while driving; do NOT do this while driving. What do you think? Anything usable for your next quilt top?

thirty eight

It's a Winner

If you entered a quilt into a show and won a big ol' cash prize, what would you spend that sweet, sweet dough on?

DESIGN AND COLOR
YOUR OWN RIBBON

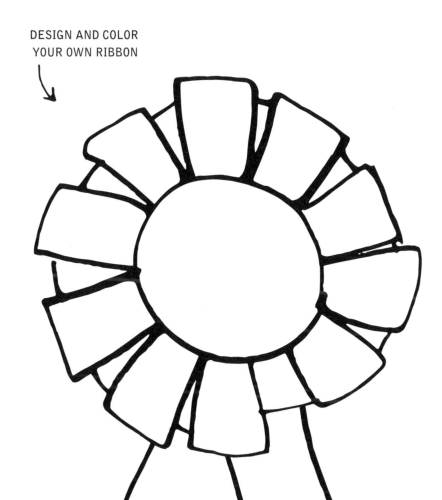

Merry Anything and Happy Quilting

Pick a holiday or season that makes you squeal with delight (test squeals aloud to confirm your top selection) and channel that love into a runner or mini quilt. Jump head first into the task of buying seasonal fabrics to make it extra special!

Swatches of my Favorite Holiday Fabrics

Attach Swatch Here

Attach Swatch Here

Attach Swatch Here

Attach Swatch Here

Attach Photo of
Quilt Here

PATTERN NAME: ....

DATE COMPLETED: ....

CIRCLE ONE: GIFTED   KEPT

You're a Natural

Go outside and sketch what you see out there. Take your time to really observe what you're looking at. Think you might be able to turn this into a quilt design, quilting design, an appliqué or embroidery? Try it here!

OK, NOW SKETCH SOMETHING QUILTY OVER HERE!

forty one

Do Yourself a Solid

No lie, bursts of colors totally make us happy. What are your top 5 favorite solids that always do the trick for you? Attach a swatch of each of them here. If you have already completed a *Quilter's Yearbook* before, compare this page with one from a previous year. Any differences or similarities?

#1. FABRIC COLOR & MANUFACTURER:

....

WHY THIS COLOR IS A FAVORITE:

....

....

....

Attach Photo Here

Attach Photo Here

#2. FABRIC COLOR & MANUFACTURER:

....

WHY THIS COLOR IS A FAVORITE:

....

....

....

[Attach Photo Here]

#3. FABRIC COLOR & MANUFACTURER:

....

WHY THIS COLOR IS A FAVORITE:

....

....

....

#4. FABRIC COLOR & MANUFACTURER:

....

WHY THIS COLOR IS A FAVORITE:

....

....

....

[Attach Photo Here]

#5. FABRIC COLOR & MANUFACTURER:

....

WHY THIS COLOR IS A FAVORITE:

....

....

....

[Attach Photo Here]

Read Not-So-Between the Lines

Have a top 10 list in your mind of specific quilting books or supplies you'd love to get your hot little hands on? List them here and then use this handy dandy bookmark as an unabashed inspirational hint and leave it where your loved ones will easily find it. Taping it to the forehead of someone near and dear to you while they sleep is an obvious option.

Hey, ...!
I know you can already read my mind, but
just as extra help, here's what's at the top of
my wishlist this year.

Your ever-helpful future gift recipient,

....

SUPPLY **#1:** ....

  APPROX. $: ....

SUPPLY **#2:** ....

  APPROX. $: ....

SUPPLY **#3:** ....

  APPROX. $: ....

SUPPLY **#4:** ....

  APPROX. $: ....

SUPPLY **#5:** ....

  APPROX. $: ....

SUPPLY **#6:** ....

  APPROX. $: ....

SUPPLY **#7:** ....

  APPROX. $: ....

SUPPLY **#8:** ....

  APPROX. $: ....

SUPPLY **#9:** ....

  APPROX. $: ....

SUPPLY **#10:** ....

  APPROX. $: ....

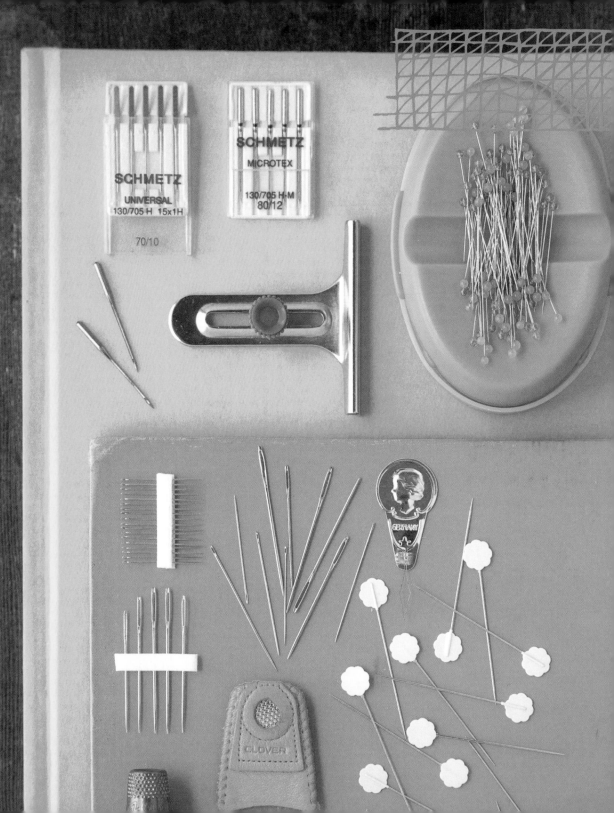

Pay It Forward

Spread the love: What would be the top 10 must-have sewing tools and notions that you'd suggest an aspiring quilter own? Next steps: Keep your eye out for these items in your daily travels and slowly gather up everything from your list. Package it all up into a fun giveaway to be hosted at your local sewing shop, community center, college, etc. to pay your sewing love forward!

The Top Tools:

#1. ....

#2. ....

#3. ....

#4. ....

#5. ....

#6. ....

#7. ....

#8. ....

#9. ....

#10. ....

PACKED UP AND GIFTED TO:

....

forty four

Something to Thank About

Not only do many hands make light work, they can also make AWESOME work, especially within the sewing community. Think about all the extraordinary folks involved—from the thread company, to the fabric designer, to the pattern maker, to the long-armer, to the book publisher—and write about how this community makes you feel. Time for a group hug!

Hear the Calling

What's the next downright irresistible fabric combination you keep thinking about test-driving? Attach swatches here!

My .... **Palette:**

WHY I LOVE THIS FABRIC COMBINATION AND POSSIBLE PLANS FOR IT:

forty five

My .... **Palette:**

THESE WOULD WORK PERFECTLY
FOR THIS PROJECT:

Good Clean Fun

Feeling uninspired? Um, unless it's a lack of sleep or even not enough caffeine (because the effects can all kinda look the same, right?!), then it could be that sewing space of yours. Let's think of 10 ways to rejuvenate that space and get you on the road to Happy Town!

Keep Calm and Get To These:

Done!

#1. ☐

#2. ☐

#3. ☐

#4. ☐

#5. ☐

#6. ☐

#7. ☐

#8. ☐

#9. ☐

#10. ☐

forty seven

Block Love

It's obvious you're bursting at the seams to scream it out, so go on, share your all-time favorite block here! What fabrics do you think would be the perfect pairing to make a spectacular quilt based on that awesome block?

My Very Favorite Block

My Fabric Plans For Making This Block

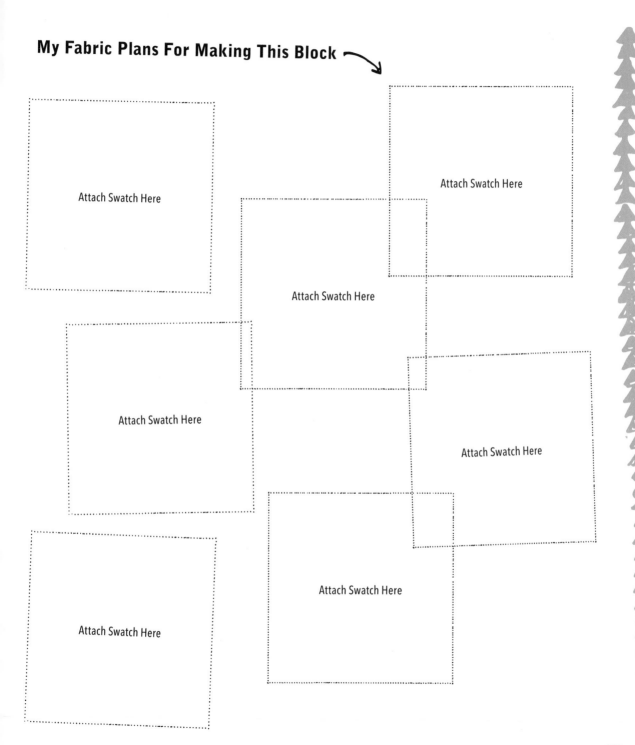

Attach Swatch Here

Attach Swatch Here

Attach Swatch Here

Attach Swatch Here

Attach Swatch Here

Attach Swatch Here

Attach Swatch Here

Get Into the Groove

Guilty quilty pleasures: Head-banging metal, punk, indie, folk, classical, operatic, whatever the ilk, list out your hands-down favorite songs to sew to. And cue the drum solo!

My Ultimate Play List:

#1. ....

#2. ....

#3. ....

#4. ....

#5. ....

#6. ....

#7. ....

#8. ....

#9. ....

#10. ....

Curator Extrordinaire

Mix-y match-y time: Choose 6 different fabrics from unrelated formal collections and create your own newly curated collection out of them. What makes them coordinate? Color? Pattern? Theme? Attach swatches of each, write about how they relate and how you'd use them together.

My Collection Name

Attach Photo Here

Attach Photo Here

Attach Photo Here

#1. FABRIC NAME:

WHY IT WORKS:

#2. FABRIC NAME:

WHY IT WORKS:

#3. FABRIC NAME:

WHY IT WORKS:

PALETTE INSPIRATION:

....

....

....

....

....

....

Attach Photo Here	Attach Photo Here	Attach Photo Here

#4. FABRIC NAME:

....

WHY IT WORKS:

....

....

....

#5. FABRIC NAME:

....

WHY IT WORKS:

....

....

....

#6. FABRIC NAME:

....

WHY IT WORKS:

....

....

....

fifty

Rules Schmools

Knowingly or unknowingly, all quilters have broken them. Write about a time when you broke the rules and what you learned. What other so-called rules are you gleefully ready to break?

RULE BROKEN: ....

PROJECT: ....

LESSONS LEARNED: ....

....

....

....

....

....

....

MY NEXT RULE-
BREAKING PLANS: ....

....

....

....

....

one

All the Heart Eyes

Boldly shout it to the rafters: what is your all-time favorite fabric?
Like, EVER?!?! Attach a swatch of it it here and let's admire it together,
shall we?

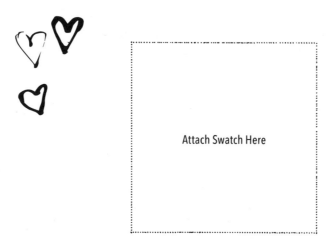

Attach Swatch Here

PRINT NAME: ....

DESIGNER: ....

COLLECTION: ....

MANUFACTURER: ....

DATE PURCHASED: ....

fifty two

Quilt of the Year

Aside from kids under the age of one and all those consecutive nightly culinary sensations you magically produce because everything you touch is gold (or at least gold-plated), attach a photo and write about the most favorite thing you've made in the last 12 months.

Attach Photo of
Quilt of the Year Here

QUILT NAME AND YEAR COMPLETED:

QUILT PATTERN: ....

SIZE: ....

QUILTED BY: ....

FABRICS USED: ....

WHAT MAKES ME LOVE THIS QUILT SO MUCH:

....

....

....

....

....

....

....

....

....

....

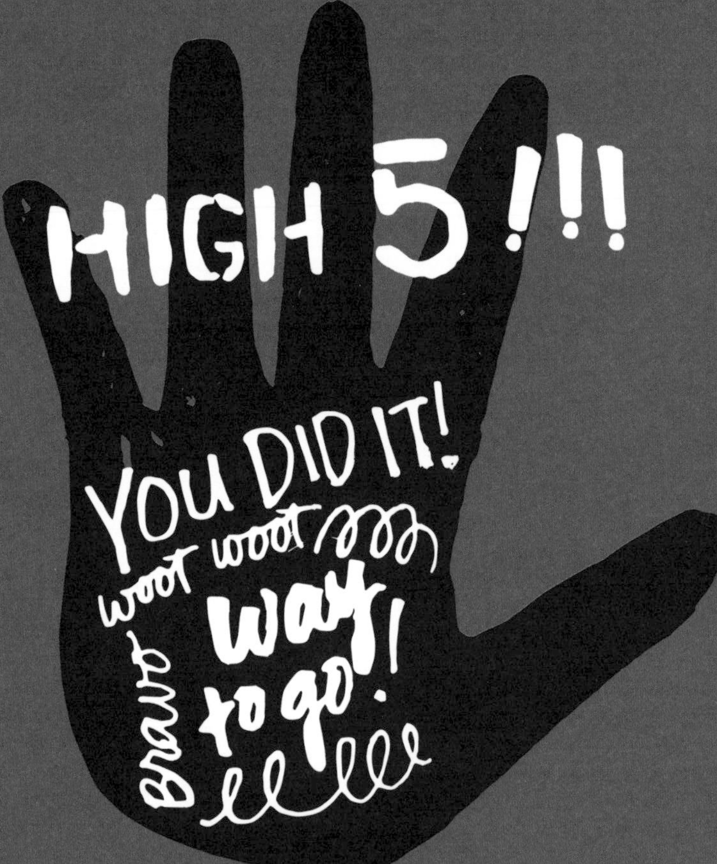
HIGH 5!!!
YOU DID IT!
woot woot
way to go!
Bravo